Science Book of VOLCANOES

With additional material on Mt. St. Helens
and Surtsey by the author

(Hardcover Title: Junior Science Book of Volcanoes)

by PATRICIA LAUBER

Illustrated with drawings by Matthew Kalmenoff

and photographs

SCHOLASTIC BOOK SERVICES
NEW YORK • TORONTO • LONDON • AUCKLAND • SYDNEY • TOKYO

ACKNOWLEDGMENTS

For assistance in checking the scientific accuracy of the manuscript, the editor and publisher are grateful to Jerry P. Eaton, geophysicist, U.S. Department of the Interior, Geological Survey.

This book was edited under the supervision of Nancy Larrick, Ed.D.

PHOTO CREDITS

COVER: Mouth of a lava stream at night, taken April 20, 1964, by Albert Jónasson; page 23, photo by Sigurdur Thorarinsson; and page 24, photo by Sigurgeir Jónasson. All are illustrations from SURTSEY: THE NEW ISLAND IN THE NORTH ATLANTIC by Sigurdur Thorarinsson. All rights reserved. Reprinted with permission of The Viking Press, Inc.

Page 4, U.S. Geological Survey; Gutierrez/UPI; page 6, Henle — Monkmeyer; page 10 (top), Stage — Photo Researchers; page 10 (bottom) and page 11, Tad Nichols; page 21, J. Titchen; page 26, Official U.S. Navy photo; page 28, Spence Air photos; page 29 (top), Japanese Information Service, (bottom), Wide World; page 33, Italian Government Travel Office; page 34, Wide World; page 35, Italian State Tourist Office; page 36, Phillips — Official U.S. Navy photo; page 41, Diller — U.S. Geological Survey; pages 42, 44, courtesy of the American Museum of Natural History; page 49, U.S. Geological Survey; page 52, Wide World; page 55, Wide World Photos; Gutierrez/UPI; page 58, Stimson — Wyoming Commerce & Industry Commission; page 59, New Zealand Information Service; page 60, National Publicity Studios, New Zealand; page 62, Monkmeyer.

Originally published and copyrighted under the title JUNIOR SCIENCE BOOK OF VOLCANOES.

ISBN: 0-590-02560-0

12 11 10 9 8 7 6 5 4 3 2   11   0 1 2 3 4 5/8

CONTENTS

(above) Mount St. Helens erupted with a bang on May 18, 1980; (below) On July 23, her 60,000-foot cloud looked like that from an A-bomb blast.

RING OF FIRE

The Pacific region has been called "The Ring of Fire" because of the many active volcanoes along its coastlines and islands.

A Volcano Is Born

THE day began like any other for a Mexican farmer named Dionisio Polido. He rose early. He had breakfast with his wife and son. Then he set out for his cornfield. He planned to spend the day clearing rocks off it.

Almost at once he discovered that this day was not just like any other. Several times he heard noises like thunder. Yet there wasn't a cloud in the sky.

Polido arrived at his cornfield. There he discovered an even stranger thing. Smoke was rising at one end of the field. Was something on fire? Puzzled, he hurried toward the smoke.

What he saw filled him with terror. The very earth seemed to be on fire. The ground had cracked open. Smoking, gray-white stuff was bubbling noisily out of the crack.

Polido felt sure the world was coming to an end. He ran to find his wife and son. The family fled to the little village of Paricutín, where Polido told of the awful sight he had seen. The terrified villagers gathered in the church.

Time passed, and nothing happened. So one of the men said, "Perhaps you made a mistake, Dionisio. Perhaps there was no smoke but only dust. Let us go and see."

Some of the men went back to the Polido farm. There they saw a terrifying sight. The earth had opened, forming a long crack. At one end was a big, pear-shaped hole. Smoke, sparks, ash, and dust poured from the hole. Red-hot stones were tossed into the air. The air itself was filled with a sharp, unpleasant smell that made the men choke.

The villagers went back to the church. Among its books they found one that told them what was happening. They had seen the birth of a volcano.

By night the volcano was roaring. Matter exploded out of it. Flashes of lightning crackled in the column of smoke and ash. A cone-shaped hill was piling up around the opening. Two days later lava started to flow from a nearby crack in the earth.

Lava buried the Polido farm and moved on, stretching out over the land. Ahead of its reach, trees died. Ash settled out of the air. Animals fled. Birds flew away. Paricutín and another village were buried. Only the church steeples showed where they had been. The Mexican government moved all the people away.

Lava from Paricutín spread out over the land and swallowed two villages. In each only the church steeple remained to show that people had once lived there.

As the lava spread, trees died and animals fled. Volcanic ash, settling out of the air, buried fields and farmhouses. The wind blew it into drifts.

Nearly all of Paricutín's growth took place during the first year. After that, minor eruptions added only a little to its height, and they came to an end when the volcano was nine years old.

The new volcano was named Paricutín for the village it destroyed. It grew and grew. Born on February 20, 1943, it grew 300 feet in the first five days. By the end of the year, it was 1,410 feet high. Then its growth slowed. In the next eight years it grew only 100 feet more. On February 25, 1952, Paricutín suddenly stopped erupting. It became one more of the quiet cones in the area.

That part of Mexico has many small volcanoes. And this is a clue to why a volcano was born in Dionisio Polido's cornfield.

What Causes Volcanoes?

A VOLCANO is an opening in the earth's crust. It is an opening where gas and rock come from inside the earth onto the surface. The rock is usually very hot — so hot that it is MOLTEN, which means "melted."

Scientists call this molten rock MAGMA. It is a special kind of rock. It contains crystals of minerals. Usually the crystals are dissolved in the hot magma, somewhat as salt or sugar dissolves in hot water. Magma also has gases in it. The gases may be dissolved in the magma or they may occur as bubbles. The chief gas is steam.

Perhaps the best way to understand magma is to compare it with soda pop.

Soda pop contains sugar. You can taste the sugar. But you do not see the crystals because they are dissolved in the liquid.

Soda pop also contains a gas called carbon dioxide. Carbon dioxide makes the bubbles in soda pop.

Suppose you take an unopened bottle of soda pop and hold it up to the light. You will not see any bubbles in it. That is because the carbon dioxide is dissolved in the liquid.

Open the bottle gently, and you see some bubbles. The gas is slowly separating out of the liquid as bubbles.

But suppose you shake the bottle before opening it. Then the gas will rush out, carrying a spray of liquid. The more violently the gas rushes out the bigger the explosion will be.

Much the same thing happens with magma when it reaches the earth's surface. If the magma is liquid, its gas may bubble out gently. Then the magma flows out quietly. If the magma is thick and sticky, the gas may separate violently. Then the magma bursts forth. The same thing may happen if the magma contains an especially large amount of gas.

The inside of an erupting volcano looks like this, with magma forcing its way up the throat and out the vents.

Either way, you say that the volcano is ERUPTING. Or you can say that a VOLCANIC ERUPTION is taking place.

Magma that has reached the surface is called LAVA. When lava cools and hardens, it can be called LAVA or LAVA ROCK.

Knowing about magma helps you understand why volcanoes erupt.

In some parts of the earth, there are pockets of magma beneath the surface. The magma presses against the rock of the earth's crust. When the magma finds a weak spot, it forces its way to the surface. That is what happened with Paricutín.

As the nearby volcanoes showed, there is magma under that part of Mexico. A crack in the rock of the crust led to Dionisio Polido's cornfield. Somehow, the magma forced its way through this crack. The crack widened into a hole. A white-hot column of magma burst through the opening. Chunks of rock were torn from the earth and hurled into the air. A volcano was born.

At first Paricutín erupted violently. Then the eruptions died down. Paricutín became the quiet, cone-shaped hill that it is today.

The hill is also called a volcano, for the word has two meanings. VOLCANO can mean the opening where magma comes onto the earth's surface. More often it means the big hill or mountain that may build up around the opening.

The hill or mountain is built of material that erupted from the opening. This material can take many forms.

What Comes Out of a Volcano?

A VOLCANO erupts when magma is forced to the surface.

As the magma cools, crystals separate out of it. If the magma cools slowly, the crystals are big. If it cools more quickly, then the crystals are smaller. If the magma cools very quickly, crystals may not form at all. Instead, the magma freezes, or hardens, into glass. Perhaps you have seen some of this natural glass. One kind is called OBSIDIAN.

Lava is usually made of glass or crystals or both.

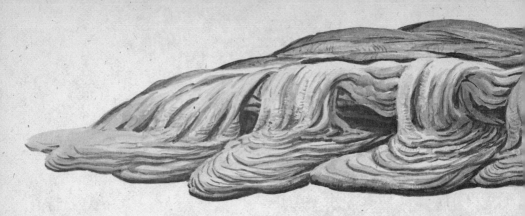

Two common types of lava flow are called by Hawaiian names, pahoehoe and aa, because they often occur on Hawaiian volcanoes. The lava flow called pahoehoe has a smooth, rolling surface.

Magma may pour out of a volcano in gentle streams called LAVA FLOWS. Or it may erupt violently because of the gas in it. The rushing gas carries along rock. Some of the rock is solid. Some is liquid. The rock is blown into the air. There the liquid rock usually hardens. All the rock falls back to earth.

Aa lava has a rough surface made of bristling fragments of lava.

There is a name for rock that is blown out of a volcano and falls to earth. The name is PYROCLASTIC (PIE-row-CLASS-tick) rock. Pyroclastic means "broken by fire."

Some pyroclastic rock is ripped loose from inside the volcano. Some is lava torn apart by the gas. The lava takes different forms. Each has its own name.

A BOMB is a rounded piece of newly hardened lava that takes its shape while flying through the air. A BLOCK is a piece of lava that has sharp corners.

Sometimes liquid lava is blown into the air. It cools there, forming coarse pieces of rock called CINDER. Cinder is bubbly rock, puffed up by gas. If it is very bubbly and puffed up, it is called PUMICE. Pumice is so bubbly that it floats in water.

Some pieces of rock are very small — the size of grains of sand. These are called ASH. Ash forms when liquid lava is blown apart by gas. When ash becomes cemented together by water it forms a rock called TUFF.

bomb

block

cinder

The smallest pieces of rock are called DUST. Some volcanic dust is very fine. A big explosion blows huge amounts of this dust high into the air. The dust particles are so small that they remain in the air for years. Volcanic dust makes itself felt in many parts of the world.

In the year 1783, for example, two volcanoes erupted violently. One was in Japan and the other in Iceland. Dust from these eruptions was so thick that it cut off some of the sun's heat. The winter of 1783-84 became one of the coldest ever recorded in North America and Europe.

pumice

tuff

In the spring of 1963, a volcano erupted on the island of Bali in Indonesia. Dust from the explosion was carried around the world. It caused bright red sunsets. Some scientists think it made a change in world rainfall patterns.

This fine dust finally settles to earth, looking like any other kind of dust. (You may have had some in your house without knowing it.) In this way, the fine volcanic dust vanishes from sight.

But other products of eruptions do not vanish. These materials build mountains. They also build broad plains called plateaus.

This car was almost buried by a rain of pumice from the volcano erupting in the background. The eruption took place in Hawaii in 1960.

Plateaus and Mountains

In the autumn of 1963 a volcano started to erupt deep in the North Atlantic. The eruptions began some 425 feet below the surface, and they soon built an underwater mountain that grew and grew.

Early in the morning of November 14, Icelandic fishermen saw columns of black smoke rising from the sea. At first they thought a ship was on fire. But, as they discovered, the smoke came from the volcano that was rising out of the sea. The volcano formed an island, later named Surtsey.

All that winter explosions added huge amounts of ash, cinder, and pumice to the new island. Stormy seas attacked Surtsey, but new material piled up faster than the sea could sweep it away.

By April the violent eruptions had stopped. Lava now flowed over the cinder and ash, forming a hard surface. Lava flowed into the sea, forming a collar that protected the island. It was clear that Surtsey had come to stay.

Surtsey, here about two weeks old, later grew to a height of 500 feet. By then the new island had an area of more than one square mile.

Lightning, generated by electrical charges in the rising material, could be seen by people in Iceland, 20 and more miles away.

The birth of Surtsey was a surprise, but the place of birth was not. Surtsey rose from a huge range of underwater mountains, called the Mid-Atlantic Ridge. The ridge is highly volcanic, and its eruptions have built many mountain peaks. The tallest ones form small islands, like Surtsey.

Outpourings of lava from the ridge also built the big island of Iceland. But in these eruptions, such as the one of 1783, lava flowed from long cracks called fissures.

In late spring of 1783 strong earthquakes shook part of southern Iceland. They were a sign that magma was moving within the earth. On June 11 the eruption began. Floods of lava poured out of a ten-mile-long crack in the earth called the Laki Fissure. Lava dried up the Skafta River and filled the riverbed to overflowing.

A week later there was another great flood of lava. A third poured forth on August 3. Lava filled what had once been a lake. It filled a huge gulf at the foot of a waterfall. Giant tongues of lava spread out over the land. They were 12 to 15 miles wide and 100 feet deep.

Finally the fissure began to choke up, and the eruption came to an end.

These giant cracks in the earth have produced the world's biggest volcanic eruptions. The biggest fissure eruptions are called FLOOD ERUPTIONS, because they pour out floods of lava. The lava is very liquid. A single flow may spread over hundreds or thousands of square miles. Such flows build plateaus, not mountains.

Rocks show that many flood eruptions have taken place in the past. Over thousands of years Iceland was built by lava floods that covered more than 200,000 square miles. The lava is about 9,000 feet thick.

Flood eruptions built big plateaus in North America. One of these is the Columbia Plateau in the northwestern United States. In places the lava rock is 5,000 feet thick. The plateau itself covers more than 100,000 square miles.

Large parts of other continents have been built in the same way. But flood eruptions do not seem to take place anymore. The 1783 eruption is the only one we have a record of.

The big eruptions we know are of a different kind. They take place through VENTS, which are pipelike openings. They build mountains, not plateaus.

Volcanic mountains have three main shapes. The shape depends on the kind of material that pours out of the vent, and on the shape of the vent.

Sometimes the material is chiefly liquid lava that pours out of long fissures in the sides of the volcano. Such eruptions build a broad, gently sloping mountain. This shape is called a SHIELD VOLCANO. It looks like a shield laid flat on the ground. Iceland has many small shield volcanoes. So do northeastern California and parts of Oregon. The Hawaiian volcanoes are shield volcanoes.

Paricutín is a different kind of volcano. This

View from the air shows the crater of this erupting volcano, off the west coast of Mexico. A crater forms when explosions blow material away from vent.

27

Sunset Crater, in Arizona, is one of the many cinder cones in the western United States. A cinder cone forms when explosions pile up cinder and ash around the vent.

Mount Shasta, in California, is a composite volcano, made of various materials. Some eruptions have added lava flows to it, while others have added cinder and ash.

Mount Fuji, Japan, is also a composite volcano. Composite volcanoes are among the world's most beautiful mountains.

Mount Etna, on the island of Sicily, was a shield volcano at first, built by lava flows. Later, violent explosions built a 1,000-foot cone on top of the shield, turning Mount Etna into a composite volcano.

kind is called a CINDER CONE. It forms when violent explosions pile up cinder and ash around the vent. A cinder cone is a large hill. It looks like a cone with the point cut off. Its top is a bowl-shaped hollow, called a CRATER.

Some cinder cones grow on the sides of bigger volcanoes. Others are found alone. There are many cinder cones in the western United States. Two examples are Sunset Crater in Arizona and Cinder Cone at Lassen National Park in California.

Some volcanoes are built both of lava flows and of ash and cinder. These are called COMPOSITE VOLCANOES. (Composite means "made of various materials.")

Composite volcanoes develop when eruptions change. For instance, a volcano may first develop as a shield volcano. Then it may start to throw out pyroclastic materials. That is what Italy's Mount Etna did. Most of the famous and beautiful volcanoes are composite volcanoes. They include Mount Hood, Mount Rainier, and Mount Shasta in the United States. Three others are Mount Fuji in Japan, Mount Mayon in the Philippines, and Popocatepetl in Mexico.

Some volcanoes, like Mount Etna, go on erupting and building for tens of thousands of years. Others, like Paricutín, become quiet. Then the question is whether they are dead or simply sleeping.

A Sleeping Giant Awakes

SOME volcanoes are known to be ACTIVE. Others are quiet and cold. They have not erupted for a very long time. These volcanoes are called EXTINCT, which means that they are "put out," or "dead." But sometimes one of these volcanoes suddenly comes alive. This shows that it was not really extinct. Rather, it was DORMANT, which means "sleeping."

The most famous dormant volcano is probably Italy's Mount Vesuvius.

Mount Vesuvius lies on the shore of the Bay of Naples, in Italy.

Two thousand years ago, Vesuvius was a green and pleasant mountain overlooking a bay. Wealthy Romans built summer homes on its slopes. Grape vines, fruit trees, and pasture grass grew in the rich soil. Towns dotted the lower slopes.

The Romans knew Vesuvius was a volcano. But they thought it was extinct. There was no record of its erupting.

In the year 63, strong earthquakes shook the region. Over the next 16 years, smaller quakes

Vesuvius grew out of an older volcano called Mount Somma, which can be seen at the left. The Romans believed the volcano to be extinct.

took place. But no one thought they were a warning.

In the year 79, the morning of August 24 dawned hot and clear. Farmers worked their fields. In the towns, people went about their work. Cooks put cakes in ovens. A grocer set out beans and grain on his counter. Someone opened a tap and water ran. A woman put away her needle and thimble in a sewing kit. Chicken was served for a noon meal. In a metal shop, a broken statue waited for repairs.

This street in Pompeii vanished with the rest of the town under a hail of ash and pumice. It was discovered and dug out only about 200 years ago.

It is still waiting. For on that day Vesuvius erupted with tremendous violence. When the eruption ended, the towns of Pompeii and Herculaneum were buried. Their daily life was frozen in time. It was still there to be seen when the buried towns were discovered nearly 1,700 years later. There were chicken bones on a table, walnuts on a snack bar, fishhooks on a line. There were houses with furniture, shops with goods, and a stage set for a play.

Pompeii was buried in ash and tiny pieces of

pumice. The pumice fell first, then the ash. Wet by heavy rains, the ash cemented into a hard layer of tuff.

Herculaneum was not in the path of the ash fall. It was buried by what is called a MUDFLOW. This is how the mudflow formed. The eruption covered the upper slopes of Vesuvius with ash, pumice, and bits of lava. Heavy rains turned this material into a kind of mud. It swept down the mountain and buried the town.

Vesuvius had proved to be a sleeping giant. Since its awakening in the year 79, Vesuvius has erupted many times. It is a mighty volcano. But other volcanoes also erupt with great violence.

In this view of Vesuvius you are looking directly into the crater.

Kinds of Eruptions

Some eruptions are gentle outpourings of lava. Some are violent explosions. There are several kinds of violent explosions.

One kind throws out chunks of older rock from inside the volcano. This kind of eruption usually takes place when steam forms suddenly. Rising magma meets water in the rocks of the earth's crust. It heats the water to temperatures above the boiling point. When the eruption begins, the water suddenly turns into steam. As a result, it expands greatly — it takes up much more space. And so an explosion takes place. That was what happened in the 1888 eruption of Bandai-san in Japan. A steam explosion blew out a whole side of the mountain. But all the chunks of rock were old. No new magma was blown out.

Another kind of explosion throws out almost nothing except new magma. That was what happened in one of the world's biggest explosive eruptions. This was the eruption of Krakatoa in 1883.

Krakatoa is an island between Java and Sumatra in Indonesia. It is an undersea volcano that has grown into an island.

In late May, 1883, explosions began in one of Krakatoa's three cones. They were not violent, and no one was alarmed. People from a neighboring island hired a steamer and visited the cone.

During the eruption of 1883, black smoke rose 17 miles into the sky over the island of Krakatoa. A giant explosion blew two of the cones to pieces with a roar that was heard 3,000 miles away. Ash and pumice darkened the sky.

The explosion threw out vast quantities of new magma from inside the earth. This seems to have undermined the volcano. Two thirds of the island of Krakatoa sank into the sea. The sinking caused a series of huge waves.

After a few days the explosions died down, then started up again.

Shortly after noon on Sunday, August 26, a huge explosion took place. It was followed by others. By two o'clock a black cloud stretched 17 miles into the sky above Krakatoa. Explosions continued through the night. The next morning, a giant explosion blew two of the cones to bits. The noise was heard more than 3,000 miles away. Ash and pumice soared miles into the air. They plunged the whole region into darkness.

Rafts of pumice blocked the water. Ships could hardly force their way through. Huge amounts of fine dust were blown high into the air. They later drifted three times around the world, causing temperatures to drop for the next two years.

All told, the explosion threw something like five cubic miles of pyroclastic material into the air. Nearly all of this material was new magma from inside the earth. Apparently this undermined the volcano. Its top sank beneath the sea. The sinking and the explosions set up huge waves. The waves drowned thousands of people on nearby islands.

Explosive eruptions have caused the tops of other volcanoes to sink in. That was what happened in the famous eruption of Mount Vesuvius. It also happened about 6,000 years ago at Crater Lake in Oregon. The sinking of the top left a hole. The hole, which has since filled with rainwater, is now a lake.

Crater Lake, Oregon, took shape some 6,000 years ago when great eruptions under-mined the top of a mountain, causing it to sink in. The resulting hole filled with rain and melting snow and became a lake, where a cinder cone forms an island.

A very different kind of eruption took place on the French island of Martinique in the West Indies.

In the spring of 1902, Mount Pelée began to stir with life. Plumes of smoke and steam drifted out of its vents. Rumblings were heard. But in the city of St. Pierre no one worried. People joked about the noises. "The old woman is grumbling again," they said.

All through April the mountain went on stirring. Ash fell like snow on St. Pierre. Puffs of wind carried it through open windows. Slight earthquakes shook dishes from the shelves.

In early May explosions were heard. Some people left the city in alarm. But others stayed. The government said there was no danger. It wanted the people to stay for an important election.

On May 5 a mudflow destroyed a sugar mill outside the city. On May 6 and 7 loud explosions were heard. Each sent a cloud of ash into the air.

Mount Pelée in eruption, December, 1902. The cloud of ash rose 13,000 feet.

This photo of the ruins of St. Pierre was taken soon after the May 8, 1902, eruption of Mount Pelée. The fire damage was caused by a mass of red-hot rock fragments at the bottom of the dark cloud that swept over the city.

Lightning crackled in the clouds.

May 8 dawned bright and sunny. A huge column of steam was rising from Mount Pelée. Two ships arrived and tied up beside the 17 others in the harbor. The decks of all were gray with ash.

At exactly 7:52 a.m. the volcano erupted violently. A great black cloud shot out of it. The cloud swept across the city toward the harbor. It seemed to clutch at the ground. Whatever it touched burst into flames. Within two minutes, St. Pierre was ablaze and some 30,000 people were dead.

In the harbor all but two of the ships were knocked over and sunk.

During the next few months, several other clouds formed. Scientists came to study them. The scientists found that the clouds shot down the mountainside at nearly 100 miles an hour. The people of St. Pierre had been killed by the blast of gases and terrible heat of the first cloud.

Then another discovery was made. At the bottom of each cloud there was a mass of red-hot, broken rock. The rock rushed along with the cloud. This kind of eruption was new to the scientists. They gave it the name GLOWING AVALANCHE.

Several glowing avalanches have taken place since 1902. For example, one rushed down Mount Lassen in 1915, destroying a forest. In 1951 another took place at Mount Lamington in New Guinea. It killed 2,000 people.

In a glowing avalanche, each piece of rock is surrounded by a shell of gas. That is why the rock can move so fast. There is almost no friction with the ground to slow it.

The same sort of thing happens in an ASHFLOW. In some eruptions gas makes magma froth violently. The magma is torn apart into ash. Each piece of ash has a shell of gas. And so the mass

This cliff is made of ignimbrite, a rock that forms when an ashflow hardens.

of ash flows freely. When the ashflow slows down and hardens, it forms a rock called IGNIMBRITE. Nevada, for example, has thousands of square miles of ignimbrite.

Eruptions of cinder and ash also form mudflows. In Iceland volcanoes sometimes erupt beneath glaciers. The melting ice turns into floods of water. The water mixes with cinder and ash, forming a mudflow. At other volcanoes the water may come from a crater lake. But most mudflows are like the one that buried Herculaneum. They form when heavy rains fall on lose cinder and ash.

Scientists have learned much about volcanoes by studying explosive eruptions. But quiet eruptions are also of great interest to them. That is why the United States has built an observatory on a live volcano in Hawaii. Our scientists want to know more about all eruptions.

Studying Volcanoes

THE Hawaiian Islands were built by undersea volcanoes. Hawaii itself is made up of five volcanoes. The volcanoes rise from the ocean floor. Their tops form the island that we see.

Two of these volcanoes have been active in recent years. They are Mauna Loa and Kilauea. Mauna Loa towers up 30,000 feet from the Pacific floor. It is the tallest mountain on earth — and it is still growing. About every five years an eruption adds more lava to it.

These volcanologists, scientists who study volcanoes, are collecting samples of gases from a cinder cone that is still hot. The masks protect them from fumes.

Mauna Loa and Kilauea erupt fairly often. But they almost always erupt gently. Lava flows quietly from long fissures, or cracks, in them. So these volcanoes are good ones to study. Scientists study them from the Hawaiian Volcano Observatory, which is built near the rim of Kilauea Crater. It is one of several volcano observatories in the world.

The scientific study of volcanoes is called VOLCANOLOGY. The scientists who study them are VOLCANOLOGISTS.

Volcanologists try to find out how volcanoes work. They study quiet volcanoes. They visit volcanoes during eruptions. They collect gases. They study rocks thrown out by volcanoes. At the observatories they keep the volcanoes under constant watch.

One of their chief instruments is the SEISMO-GRAPH. It records the light earthquakes caused by magma moving beneath a volcano. Another instrument is the TILTMETER. It shows when the earth's surface is tilting because magma is welling up into a volcano. Hawaiian volcanoes, for instance, swell before an eruption. Once the eruption begins, they shrink.

The seismographs and tiltmeters tell volcanologists what is going on inside the earth. They give clues to an eruption, like the one at Kilauea Iki, a crater on Kilauea.

For several years there had been no big eruption at Kilauea. Then in October, 1958, seismographs recorded light earthquakes. This was a sign that magma was moving. By spring, tiltmeters showed that the mountain was beginning to bulge near the crater.

In the middle of summer the swelling went down. But on August 14, a swarm of small earthquakes took place. Their starting point was 35 miles below Kilauea. The quakes meant that magma was moving through channels that led into the mountain. The mountain began to swell.

By early November, the mountain was swelling three times as fast. On November 14, the quakes became ten times stronger. Magma was tearing rock apart. Lava broke out along a half-mile-long fissure in Kilauea Iki. The quakes stopped, but the ground rocked as lava streamed up through the newly opened fissure.

Lava poured out into the crater. Soon it was 335 feet deep. The eruption stopped, began again, and stopped. This time the lava ran back down its vent, like water draining out of a bathtub.

From then until December 21, 14 fountainlike eruptions took place. One squirted glowing lava 1,900 feet into the sky. Yet lava kept running back down the vent. Tiltmeters showed that the mountain was bursting at the seams. Something would have to give way.

A clue soon came. It was another swarm of small earthquakes. A seismograph showed that the source of the quakes was moving steadily eastward. Volcanologists tracked the quakes to the village of Kapoho, 30 miles from the crater.

From an airplane it was possible to see the long streams of molten lava spilling down the sides of Kilauea and forming the lava lake below.

On January 13, 1960, the village began to shake. Its people were warned to leave.

By evening, part of the land had sunk several feet. The whole area rocked. Just after dark there was a great roar. A three-quarter-mile-long fissure opened beside the town. Fountains of glowing lava soared into the sky.

The eruptions lasted 36 days. Lava flows swallowed houses, stores, farmland. But thanks to the warning, no one was hurt or killed.

The lava of Hawaiian volcanoes is thin and fluid. That is why it flows readily and erupts gently. Scientists can trace its movements and measure what is happening. They can tell when and where an eruption will take place.

The lava flows engulfed the homes and stores of Kapoho.

Many other volcanoes have thick, sticky lava. When one of these begins to stir, its lava may plug the vent so that pressure builds up inside. No one can be sure if the volcano will erupt at all. But if it does, it is likely to explode — and that was what happened with Mount St. Helens, in the Cascade Range.

St. Helens was one of a chain of dormant volcanoes reaching from northern California to southern British Columbia. In March, 1980, St. Helens awoke from a 123-year sleep. It shook with small earthquakes. On March 27, the volcano made a loud noise and started to give off steam and gas. Ash stained its snow-covered slopes. For weeks St. Helens went on stirring. There were signs that magma was forcing its way up into the mountain. In April, scientists discovered a big bulge growing fast on the north slope.

All this time, scientists were measuring the changes taking place in Mount St. Helens. They understood what was happening, but there was no way to tell what the volcano would do next.

Early on May 18, the trapped gases exploded

(above) Mount St. Helens, once snow-capped and serene above Spirit Lake. (below) Her blasted-out crater, erupting in July, 1980. Mount Hood is in the distance.

with a bang that was heard 300 miles away. They blew the whole top off the mountain. Ash, rock, dust, steam, and gas blasted miles into the air. Masses of material roared down the mountain. Huge mudflows followed, as ash mixed with melting snow. Before them, forests of tall trees fell like matchsticks. Rivers boiled and overflowed. Ash blanketed large parts of Washington, Oregon, Idaho, and Montana. Some lives were lost, but many more were saved because of the warnings of scientists.

Within a month, Mount St. Helens erupted twice more. No one could tell how long the eruptions would go on. In the past, St. Helens erupted for 20 or 25 years at a time. Scientists could only go on studying the volcano, learning from it, and watching for signs of danger. They also kept watch on other volcanoes in the Cascades. At least two were showing signs of wakening from their long sleeps.

Volcanoes and Man

No one can stop a volcano from erupting. But volcanologists are learning to tell when and where an eruption will take place. They are learning also to tell what kind of an eruption the volcano will produce. They are hoping to learn how to control lava flows, mudflows, and gases. As they learn, they can better protect people who live near active volcanoes. And that is just where many of the world's people live.

Perhaps you wonder why anyone would live near an active volcano. Some have no place else to live. And there is still another reason — volcanoes

Old Faithful, the famous geyser of Yellowstone National Park, Wyoming. A geyser is a special type of hot spring that erupts from time to time. Old Faithful won its name because people can count on it to erupt more often than any of the other big geysers in the Park.

have given man several gifts. The greatest of these is fertile soil. Volcanic ash supplies minerals that plants need to grow well. Some volcanic regions are among the most fertile in the world. And so people have clustered in them.

Volcanoes also supply steam and hot water in some parts of the world.

You have probably heard of hot springs. They are found where heat from magma turns ground water into hot water.

Natural underground steam has been harnessed to produce electricity at Wairakei, on New Zealand's North Island.

Yellowstone National Park has about 3,000 hot springs. No volcano has erupted there for thousands of years. But magma is still cooling near the surface. Its steam heats the ground water, which bubbles out as hot springs.

Many health resorts are built around hot springs. People believe that bathing in the springs is good for the health.

Icelanders long ago put their natural hot water to work. They piped it into greenhouses, where they grew vegetables, flowers, and fruits. Today natural hot water heats schools, hospitals, and many houses there.

Areas of bubbling mud at Wairakei, as at Yellowstone, are caused by steam rising in the mud and forming bubbles, which burst.

In some volcanic regions, steam is tapped and used to generate electric power.

This was first done in Italy, near Larderello, in the late 1800's. Wells are driven 500 to 1,500 feet into the ground. There they tap into natural steam vents. The steam is used to power the generators that produce electricity.

Larderello also supports a large chemical industry. The chemicals come from gases taken out of the steam. The chief chemical is boric acid.

In the United States a natural steam plant produces electricity at The Geysers, in Sonoma County, California. More plants are being planned. Mexico, New Zealand, Japan, the Soviet Union, and the Philippines also have power plants that use natural steam.

Making use of volcanoes is a very good reason for studying them. Scientists have still another. Volcanoes are windows in the earth. They are a clue to what goes on below the surface, in parts of the earth that we never see. An understanding of volcanoes will help us to understand the earth on which we live.

INDEX

Kilauea Iki's fountains of glowing lava attracted thousands of visitors in 1959.